ENDORSEMENTS FOR THE JESUS MOMENTS SERIES

"Jesus is always far better and far more interesting than we think he is, and seeing how the Old Testament points to him is a great way to find out how. These wonderful books will help us see more and more of Jesus."
SAM ALLBERRY, Associate Pastor at Immanuel Church, Nashville;
Author of *Why Bother with Church?* and *James For You*

"When we teach children that the stories from the Old Testament culminate in Christ, they begin to understand that he is the center of the Bible's story. This series highlights Jesus, the hero of every Bible story, and encourages readers to keep him at the center of their stories too."
HUNTER BELESS, Founder and Host of the Journeywomen podcast;
Author of *Read It, See It, Say It, Sing It*

"I smiled from ear to ear. My daughters came alive when they caught on. Hidden in this engaging true story is another *even more exciting*. We flipped backward and forward, all the while learning the biblical story and freshly encountering Christ."
DAVID MATHIS, Senior Teacher and Executive Editor at desiringGod.org;
Pastor of Cities Church, Saint Paul; Author of *Rich Wounds*

"We want our kids to see that the Old Testament points to Christ. In her marvelous *Jesus Moments* series, Alison Mitchell helps children seek-and-find the Old Testament connection to Jesus in fun ways they'll be sure to remember!"
DANIKA COOLEY, Author of *Bible Investigators: Creation; Bible Road Trip*™
and *Help Your Kids Learn and Love the Bible*

"Alison Mitchell draws children into a rich, true way of reading the Old Testament. The books are fresh, lively, attractive, intriguing and thought-provoking. Warmly recommended."
CHRISTOPHER ASH, Author and Writer-in-Residence at Tyndale House, Cambridge

"This *Jesus Moments* series is a delight! The clear and plain teaching of God's word, coupled with the intriguing illustrations and cleverly hidden symbols, make these books a win-win!"
MARY K. MOHLER, President's wife at SBTS in Louisville, Kentucky; Founder and Director of Seminary Wives Institute; Author of *Growing in Gratitude*

"What a clever series! By using symbols that children must find and explore, these books draw out significant links between Old Testament characters and Jesus. Perfect for parents and teachers who want to help their children understand God's big story."
BOB HARTMAN, Author of *The Prisoners, the Earthquake, and the Midnight Song*
and YouVersion's *Bible App for Kids*

Jesus Moments: David
© The Good Book Company 2024

Illustrated by Noah Warnes | Design & Art Direction by André Parker | All rights asserted

"The Good Book For Children" is an imprint of The Good Book Company Ltd
North America: thegoodbook.com UK: thegoodbook.co.uk Australia: thegoodbook.com.au
New Zealand: thegoodbook.co.nz India: thegoodbook.co.in

ISBN: 9781784989408 | JOB-007472 | Printed in India

Jesus Moments

David

Finding Jesus in the story of David

Written by **Alison Mitchell**   Illustrated by **Noah Warnes**

Did you know that the oldest stories in the Bible are a bit like puzzles? If you look carefully, you can spot some

"Jesus moments".

These are moments when someone in the story is a little bit like **Jesus**.

So this book is the exciting true story of how a young shepherd called **David** became a king. But what makes it even more exciting is that it's also about **Jesus**, the King of all kings.

As you read about **David**, keep a lookout for some hidden **crowns**. Each time you spot one, that's a clue that there's a **Jesus moment** to find as well.

So let's get started...

"**Wow!**" thought Samuel, as he looked at the tall, handsome man standing before him.

"Surely this is the man the Lord has chosen to be king."

God had told Samuel that one of the sons of Jesse would be the next king of God's people, the Israelites. But it wasn't this one...

"You are looking at him in the wrong way," God said. "I don't look at the outside – at how strong or handsome someone is. I look at the inside. I see their **heart** – whether or not they love me and want to live for me. I have not chosen this man."

So Samuel looked at the next son, and the next one, and the next and the next and the next and the next...

But God hadn't chosen any of them. Now there was only one left – the youngest, David, who looked after the sheep.

David was young but also fit and strong — and just as good-looking as his older brother! But that wasn't where God was looking. God could see David's heart. He knew that David loved him and wanted to live for him. **"Yes,"** said God to Samuel. "This is the one I have chosen."

So Samuel **anointed** David by pouring some oil on David's head. This meant that David had been chosen as God's king.

But David wasn't king yet...

Saul was king.

Saul was in charge of leading the Israelites in battle.
But a huge, scary army of Philistines was attacking!
They had an **enormous** champion called **Goliath.***

No one was brave enough to fight Goliath. David's older
brothers wouldn't fight him. None of the other soldiers
would fight him. Even the king, Saul, wouldn't fight him.

Goliath was laughing at God's people, and he was insulting God. That made David very angry.

"I will fight him," said David.

So he took his sling, and five stones, and went to fight the giant.

* You can read the whole story in the Bible in 1 Samuel 17.

David ran towards Goliath, twirling his sling above his head.

The first stone flew fast and straight, whistling through the air, and hit Goliath right in the middle of his forehead. Goliath rocked backwards, sideways, forwards... and fell down on his face.

And just like that, the giant was **dead**.

David didn't look like he would win. But he did. Why?
Because he was the king God had chosen for his people,
and he knew that God would help him to **save his people**
from their enemies.

King Saul wouldn't fight Goliath. But David **loved** God and wanted to **live for him**. He trusted God to help him. Which of them do you think was the kind of king who would please God?

When the army returned from beating the Philistines, the people came out to meet them. "Saul wins against thousands of men – but David wins against tens of thousands!" they sang. This made Saul very jealous. "They will try to make David king instead of me," he thought. So he tried to kill David...

Once, Saul threw a **spear** at David. He missed, and David got away.

After that Saul and his soldiers chased David up hills... down valleys... and through the wilderness. But David always escaped.

And then David had an opportunity to kill Saul...

David was hiding in a cave when Saul came in.

"Let's kill him!" said David's men. "Then you can be king in his place." David crept up behind Saul and cut a piece from his cloak... but then he slipped away again without hurting Saul.

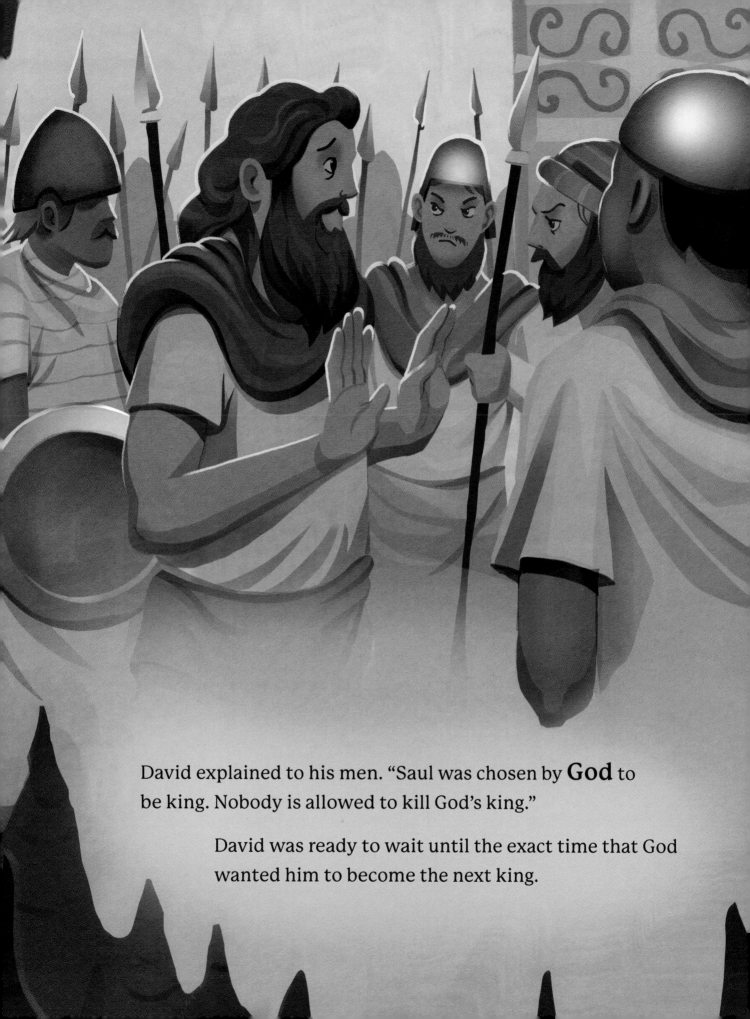

David explained to his men. "Saul was chosen by **God** to be king. Nobody is allowed to kill God's king."

David was ready to wait until the exact time that God wanted him to become the next king.

Eventually, King Saul died. At last, David became the king of all of Israel, just as God had promised. The people were able to settle peacefully in their homes, and David lived in a beautiful palace.

"But this is not right," he thought. "Surely God should have a beautiful home too! I shall build him a temple."

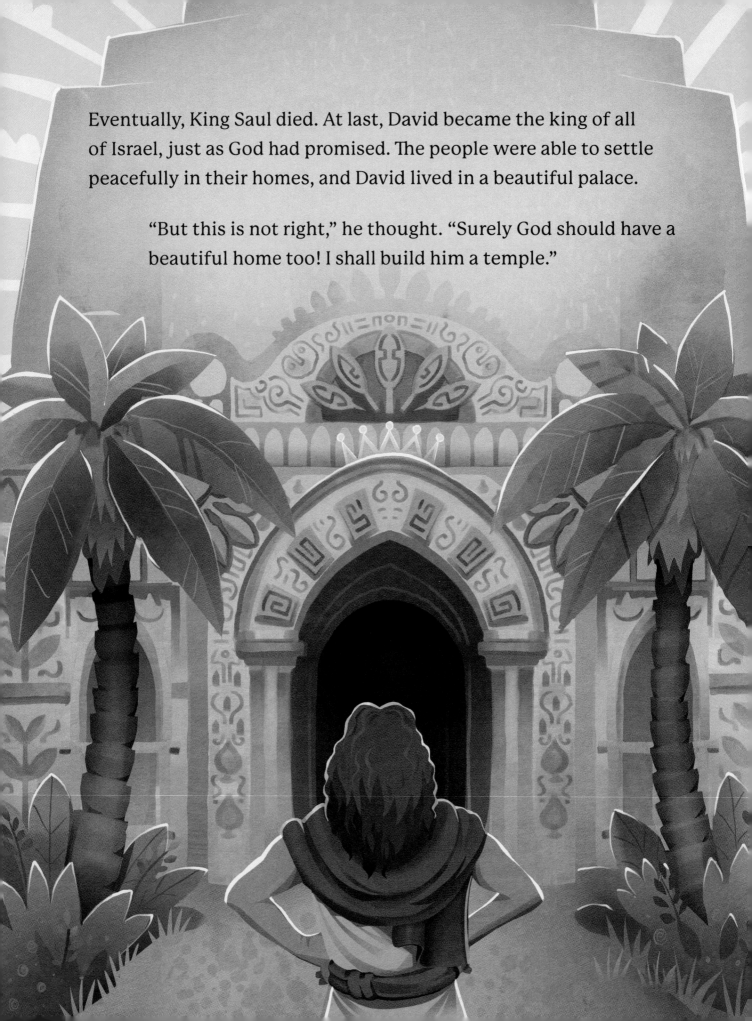

But God didn't want to **get** something from David – he wanted to **give** something to David. A promise.

"You are a great king, but you will die," God told him.
"But I promise that one day, someone from your
family will be King of my people for ever and ever."

Now it's time to spot some **Jesus moments.**

Look back at the pictures in the book. Did you spot the special **crowns?** They appear every time there is a Jesus moment in the story.

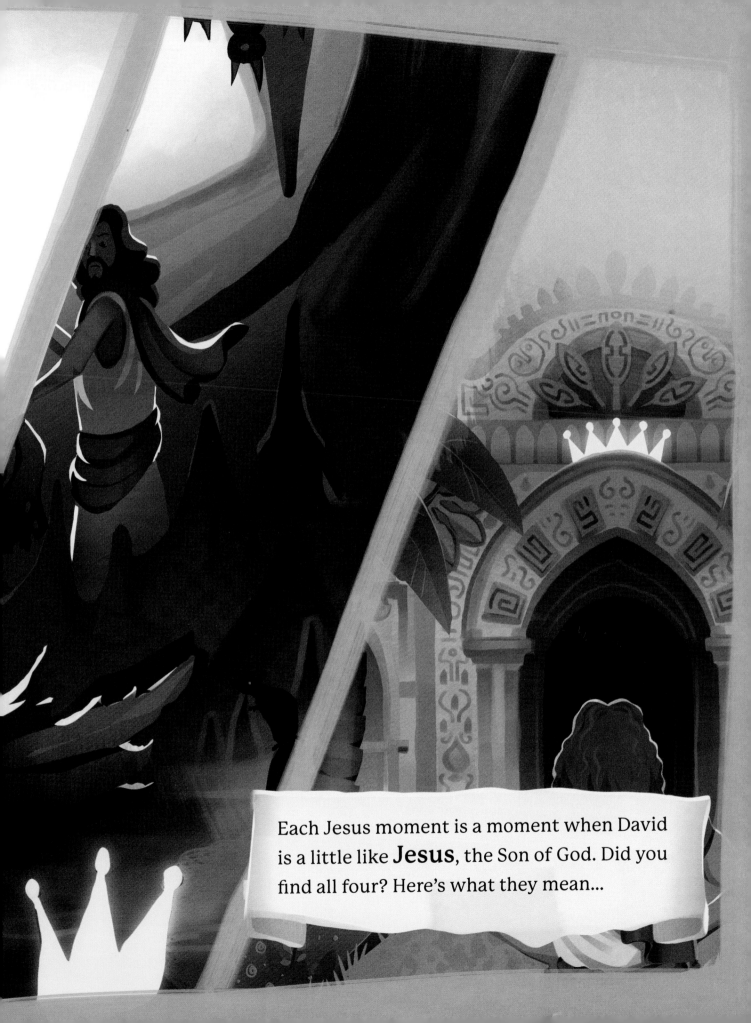

Each Jesus moment is a moment when David is a little like **Jesus**, the Son of God. Did you find all four? Here's what they mean...

David was **anointed** with oil to show that God had chosen him to be king.

Jesus is sometimes called Jesus Christ, or Jesus the Messiah. The names "Christ" and "Messiah" both mean **"the anointed one"**. They are titles that show that Jesus is God's chosen King.

David didn't look like he would beat Goliath. But he trusted God to help him **save God's people** from their enemies.

When Jesus was nailed to a cross, he didn't look like a winner either. But he knew that dying on the cross was the only way to **save God's people** from sin.

David could have killed Saul, but he chose not to,
even though Saul was his **enemy**.

When Jesus was on the cross, he prayed for his **enemies**. He asked his Father, God, to forgive them for killing him. And then he said, "It is finished", and he died.

God promised David that someone from his family would be **King** for ever.

Who was that **King?** Yes, that's right. It was **Jesus!**
But Jesus died, so how could that be?

Jesus really did die on the cross. But he didn't stay dead. God brought him back to life for ever. Jesus is still alive today – and he is ruling as **King**.

Jesus welcomes everyone who comes to him as their King. If we ask him, he will give us a heart that loves God and wants to live for him.

What would you like to say to him now?

Why look for "Jesus Moments"?

The oldest parts of the Bible were written hundreds or even thousands of years before Jesus was born, and yet they all point to him! And when we read the accounts of many Old Testament characters, we can see moments when they are a little bit like Jesus himself.

These "Jesus moments" help us to see Old Testament stories afresh and to understand more deeply who Jesus is and why he came.

The Old Testament story of David is very long. It runs from 1 Samuel 16 all the way to 1 Kings 2. We have only touched on a few parts of his life in this storybook. If you read the full Bible account, you will spot other "moments" when something in the life of David pointed towards the life of Jesus Christ, the Son of God.

It was always God's good plan to send his Son to live on Earth, to die for our sins and then to rise to life again. And God gave his people lots of clues about how this would happen.

The risen Jesus told his followers that the Old Testament Scriptures are about him: "And beginning with Moses and all the Prophets, he explained to them what was said in all the Scriptures concerning himself" (Luke 24 v 27). So when we read exciting Old Testament stories, we can look out for those same clues – those "Jesus moments" that point to the even more exciting story of Jesus himself.